She Asked Me Where

KATIE HOLTMEYER

POEMS

I.

ACKNOWLEDGEMENTS

Many thanks to the publications in which the following poems first appeared.

"The Hardest Part" –Words & Whispers

"Independent Detonations" – Superfroot Magazine

"Liar" – 3 Moon Magazine

"Confetti Cups" – Jupiter Review

"Golden Safety" – Pocketfire Poetry

"Country Curtains" – Stanchion Zine

"Cadavers" – The Shore

I.

SHE ASKED ME WHERE SHE COULD POSSIBLY GO FROM HERE

she knew more about the world at thirteen
than I do now but I still dug into
my pockets to find some advice hidden among the
quarters and gum tucked into their linings

I said don't you ever forget
you've got fire in your hands
and springs in your feet you're
gonna be somebody someday
because you already are

those days are dark but they're getting fewer
and farther between
lean into finding out
your roots are yours alone
don't bend them slice them
destroy them for a wish

I told her there's something to be said
for how when you google
"violent young female characters"
google asks if you meant

not violent but "bold" or
"empowering" or "strong"
and I'm not sure if that means google
doesn't understand what a violent girl is
or if google knows what a girl is
best of us all

and she told me about the names
the guys at school had called her
and all I could do was offer her
some gum
and a couple quarters

POWDER BLUE FLUSH

I've been looking for something since
the day I turned fifteen but
I still haven't found it yet

I'm beginning to wonder
if I should call off the search
I've been trying to drink more water
to eat more vegetables
I've been giving myself so many haircuts

I'm not wanting to be wretched
but I bought a pair of rose gold
scissors so I could feel pretty
when I hurt things

and when I say I don't trust you what I mean is
that I do but I don't want you to know
you have that kind of power over me

we are all over each other's memories
and the reality is there are only so many
reasons people run toward the things they
know could kill them

you can tell a lot about a person by the pages
they earmark in collections and the phrases
they underline in fiction

honey, the opposite of nostalgia
is knowing you'd never go back even if it meant
a hand to hold or well-meaning ignorance

but that doesn't mean the summer isn't full of it
sitting on hot rocks in our swimming suits
the beauty of an empty body
of water the possibilities
that come without gravity

but shiver, honey, we're in winter
and we'll joke about all that's fucked up
around us so they'll never guess there's more to tell

when I sleep now I dream of a different hell
in this one you are with me at least

how do you spend
a makeshift eternity?

here are my chipped nails cutting
into my palms
clutching a tangled rosary

I am on both ends of the spectrum
of so many things

something like a security blanket
within dark lipstick and a little yellow pill

here I am on my knees
take that as you will

PAPER NAILS

tonight there are four stars seeped in navy blue
which doesn't feel like enough

I've been crying glitter
for as long as I can remember
but these days that doesn't mean much

I asked you to meet me in the graveyard past sunset
so I could remind myself why I needed to stop
caring how your day went

but I'm still playing
with the loose strings on my jeans
and you're growing exasperated

there's a layer of mud caked on the bottom
of my knockoff dr. martens and somehow
even our metaphors are dead

I've beheaded all the grass left around us
so I say what I came to admit:
you deserve someone who deserves you
and I am too much work to be worth it

this is where I thought I'd tell you
not to argue
please don't be sad

but you're standing up and
now I can see there was never any need
for that

you're gone already

and I'm still playing
with the loose strings on my jeans

HALF A WATER TOWER

the amber sweatshirt I wore today
for the first time this season
still gives the slightest scent of bonfire
despite the times I've washed it
and the layers of cotton and denim
it's been buried beneath

I guess glory never quite leaves
once it's made its presence known
and whatever comes after couldn't matter against
the edge of begging and forgetting
of tripping over our tendencies
getting caught up in new pocketknives and pepper sprays
and spitting fireball onto open flames

I couldn't give up the ghost I never had
him in the first place

we all want to believe we are capable of
balancing between danger and destruction
like tightrope walking the steel beam
of a bridge half a water tower tall

imagine an icarus whose story ended
before the fall

finds its theme in the scratches on my knees
from running between the trees and
unafraid from bar to bar

but the thing about keeping your balance
is that it's hardest to do in the dark

and when the streetlights break
you're left alone to cope with your mistakes
something as sad as a voicemail message
or a dredged lake

no exchange policy no one there
to plead your case to help you take it back

when you shatter a beer bottle on the sidewalk on purpose
you don't get to bleed when you step on the glass

you are there
in an abandoned alley
with the flashlight on your phone
searching desperately
for some three-year-old graffiti

to remind you
you once left your mark on something

REFRIGERATOR MAGNETS

there's evidence of you everywhere
tucked in the back of my drawers
slightly off their hinges and always getting trapped
wadded up in leftover wrapping paper peppered
with snowflakes and santas tangled
up in the dust bunnies lining the corner
where the cabinet meets the floor
and we all know how fast dust bunnies multiply

it's a perpetual kick to the peripheral gut
when I find you in the junk bin
and in the pocket of my winter coat
and by the champagne corks I collected
before I got tired of popping them
over and over and over again
the day I stopped holding my breath
while I held the bottle in one hand
over the kitchen sink

you're rolled up tightly in my rubber bands
and buried in a sandbox hidden
in the cookie jar I never
even put any cookies in

because it seemed silly to
not just leave them in the package
it seemed silly to
do the extra work
to take you off the refrigerator
toss you out of the shower
flip past you on the calendar

so I left it hanging there
a permanent november

I left the turkey in the freezer
frozen

PILLOW SHAMS

I lied—I didn't go out last night
I drove around until I found
a parking lot by a store
with no lights on
I lied—I read the mail you threw out
the junk I knew you didn't care about
I know you'd rather not have
the headache and I should
say *I lied* here
for consistency's sake
but consistency is for cowards
and academic papers
and I didn't lie this time
not now not the start
don't understand why
truth is just the one part
you'll come around again
soon I'm sure but for now
just know what I told you
about the guy who
walked me home that night
was all I had to say
it's useless to tell you when you lie

all the time
no one believes you
you were the boy who warned
of the wolves in your town
and I was the joker who spent all
my words on punchlines
until when I tried to cry
about the wolves inside me
everyone slapped their knees
and when I reiterated
the way I felt like a mattress
with a sheet that didn't fit it
they told me
they didn't get it

THE HARDEST PART

pick up the phone with blurry eyes and barely recognize
the voice that's speaking say please, Grandma, breathe
you're scaring me you know
I wouldn't let anything or anybody hurt you
there's not much you can do you forget how scary it is
when she talks to the air
addresses people that aren't there
can't seem to remember when or where
until the good moments come sprinkled in like clarity
but she was just here but she was but she's not now
she's squinting she's looking around
trying to figure her surroundings out
trying to remember her own house
trying to fit you now
into a time in her life from before you were even born like
starting out with the skeleton of one puzzle and trying
to finish with pieces from a different box
she can't just she can't just turn it off
no matter how much I want her to
the second guessing, hesitating, pausing
between words so long the spaces fill the room

until you can't breathe until
you can't see her struggling
so you snap

because you forgot for a second
that she can't help it that she's not who she used to be
pull yourself together and remember all she's done
take a breath take her hand hold her gaze
point to the pictures and say
this is your daughter your nephew your friend
this is your grandson your husband your cousin this is me
this is me this is me please don't forget
there's so much to hold onto but the rope's wearing thin
and each exchange is important
find myself nodding along smoothing over the gaps
she's created in our conversations
acting like I understand her narration
because if I don't
our talks would be a long list of no's and nobody wants that
and I'd call every week
say I'm just checking to see how she is
is she happy did she eat is she comfortable did she sleep
does she still remember me
this new memory's
a monster only I can't open the closet door
pick the comforter up off the floor

prove to myself it isn't there because
the scariest monsters are usually the ones you can't see
don't even know how to grieve there's no seven steps
to follow for the death of a memory

want to beg scream plead
don't you remember who you are?

don't you remember how you'd make me breakfast in bed so
one day I said I'd do it for you too
got up early fixed your coffee except I was too young then
to know the difference between regular and instant
so you took a big sip got a mouthful of grounds
and you spit them out and I almost cried
but you smiled and we tried again

don't you remember how kind you are?
the stories you used to tell? please don't yell
you're not mean like this you're not angry like this
you're not

don't you remember who you are?

some days I start to think you do
and other days I leave the room
because you seem like an imposter walking

in my grandma's shoes and on those days
I don't know whether the hardest part
is that you don't remember

or whether the hardest part
is that I do

INDEPENDENT DETONATIONS

a ghost plays kick the can over on first street
and a song you sent me years ago
crackles behind the explosions

I prep a bottle for a rocket
bite a sparkler between my teeth

I'm not naïve enough to think
we could have had forever but
a little longer would have been nice

people come into your life then they leave
and they don't take enough with them

what we had was fun and neither of us
broke it—this is just the way things work out
sometimes

call it good
call it passing by
call it a magic trick since those only last
as long as you are willing to not look too closely

I will try not to let you into the lineup
of everyone who might come next
but I've gotten into a terrible habit
of breaking my intentions

the wind dusts my hair with ashes
I put the sparkler out
on my skin

STEEL FLAMES

so this is where we end
trespassing on a dock
by a midnight pond
by this I mean I kissed
your favorite wristwatch
threw it in the black water
and made the sign of the cross

for them, then, I sit with their disbelief
belly empty save some stolen sips of warm beer
I want to be quiet in my grief
but it is so loud in here

I should be relieved, see, so many
of my secrets are safe with you
in a coffin underneath the salty mud

I have nothing to be ashamed of
except for everything I've ever done

my friend, I won't pour one out for you
I know you wouldn't want me to waste
perfectly good whiskey

each moment I miss the bravery you gave me
the way ice can always be lurking beneath the snow
the way fire doesn't give a fuck what it burns

what comes after hell?

CARELESS HANDS

I used to wonder how many bones were
resting at the bottom of the ocean and
why emotions have to be so damn scary

the way I missed the weight of
your body on top of me but I
never missed what came next

never replicated that look
in your eyes in mine but
I will still blame you because
I can't stand to blame myself

you asked what you did wrong
and I didn't know what to say because
you never stood a chance in the first place

I didn't save our ticket stubs
never waited up for your texts
this nicotine tastes like regrets but
it's steady between my two fingers

I'll take another sip of sangria we all know
God wouldn't make a fruit this sweet

truth be told I still wonder what's
buried in the sand

meet me in the dark by the trains again
you should've pushed me when
you had the chance

SCRATCHED MARKS

no one wants to see the ways
we cope when we're alone
lying on the carpet clawing at my skin

thinking about all the ends all that might
destroy me like the withdrawing of what
I thought I had and panic and pain and conflict
and sometimes something simple like
spilling cereal or a gillete commercial

sometimes the lullaby where the baby
who cries too much falls out of the tree
except I am the tree

but mostly the memory of all the moments
I wasted like that phase when she was
whiplash and fear of clinging and bargaining

she was a caricature of someone else she was
herself she was a rotation of kindness and
confusion of love and anger in uneven fits and
there's a metaphor here about jekyll and hyde but
it feels wrong to reach for it

spent too much time exhausted at lost puzzle pieces
and cold coffee the aching of feet and the numbness
of a lack of sleep give me all those minutes
I lay awake back I need to get up

tell me a story about a girl who never
thought she'd have to show her grandma
how to use the bathroom

she tried to find a loophole a rewrite
another chapter but once the ink dries
no one gets to decide they don't like the ending

and you can search between the words for themes
and hidden meanings for redemption arcs and
reliving and some kind of mandatory allegory but
I guess the moral of the story is

I never did learn the moral
of that story

THERE ARE NO WINDOWS IN THIS BATHROOM

the other day the automatic light
didn't come on
when I walked into the bathroom
and I wondered if I was invisible
I know
I'm not invisible
but I guess sometimes the ground I walk on
feels like one of those trap
doors on game shows that
opens up to swallow you whole
when you get the answer wrong
and usually it feels like I'm getting the answer wrong
even when everything tells me I'm getting it right it's like
the light still isn't coming on
when I walk into the bathroom and
when I get back to my room I'll sit and assume
I've done something wrong again
something's wrong again
I've mentioned my anxiety three times today and
that makes me anxious
sometimes it feels like my mind
is made up of scars and when one

of my fears is confirmed
all of them are
feels like a bar
is lying against my chest sometimes
and with each breath
my lungs have to bench press
to keep me alive
the first time I went to counseling
I apologized to my therapist
for crying in his office
and wondered if he thought I was overly emotional
I'm always asking questions
supplying my own medicine and sense
of self is so screwed up it always feels like
I'm getting the answer wrong again
something's wrong and I wish
I didn't feel invisible
when the light doesn't come on

ON A MONDAY AT 5:30 IN THE AFTERNOON

if we'll be walking in concentric circles
please don't stand on my left side
you'd think I've got an affinity for
long flannels and ponytail holders
but truth is I've just been playing this
game of hide and seek for so long

please, are you angry?
I'm no stranger to I'm sorry
and nothing changes after a tragedy
except everything

all I wanted all summer was to climb just one tree
perched and able to skim and see freedom
written in the falling stars for me
but the branches must have cracked under
the weight of my drowning

scraped my shins on the way down
both of them
left my skin raw
like the exposed wood beneath the carpet

they cut away from your bedroom floor

I am sorry
for always apologizing in my poems
I am sorry
I know you used to say without me
in your life you would kill yourself but
I never thought you'd make good on that promise

there are a million ways to say
what we don't mean
sometimes I bring broken things
I could fix myself to my dad
and ask my mom questions
I already know the answer to

I'm walking on new street now and the
snow flurries are refusing to hit the ground
like there's no safe space to land
so I hold out my hand to catch them
and wonder if the people driving by know
I am dreaming of a poem

I've got so many empty notebooks filled
with words I never wrote

sometimes the sirens go off so often
I forget to be sad when I hear them

I am always mistaking insomnia
for inspiration

hey, I got through another twelve hours today
maybe tomorrow will be a little better
than this maybe I should go to confession
again maybe I should kiss a stranger and pretend
to be who the world assumes I am for a while

anything to stop myself from going down
one more damned rabbit hole

I'm sorry
I've studied chekov's gun
I should have seen it coming

I could recreate every popcorn mark
on my bedroom ceiling

I've been sinking
since summer

and the branch is still breaking

MORNING COFFEE

she told me that when she
was a toddler she was
afraid of four things
toasters
gas stations
mascots
and her dad
she tailored her life
to work around them
understanding that
this was no way to live
she mentioned to me
she stopped trying to avoid
what made her feel like dying
and instead
charged head-first into chaos
you can tell she did this
by the way she never
seems afraid of dark streets
or memories
electricity in lightning storms
or the pills she finds

on bathroom floors
she tosses another back
and tells me courage
should always override caution
but when no one's looking
in the morning
she still flinches
when the toast pops up

TEPID

I left a glass of wine
half-drunk
on the edge of the bathtub

and I left you
standing there

blew out the candle on my way so
I wouldn't have to see
the contours of your face
as they changed
wouldn't have to look at myself
in the still-clear mirror

maybe I'll find you
in every song I listen to
or maybe I'll forget
we ever met

our story started with memories
our future already before
we tinged and tainted it
with what we did

all that we can't take back

and when you kissed me it tasted like
a conversation I didn't want to have

the curve of your spine like
a question mark

maybe I'll keep asking
what's wrong with me with us

maybe I'll always get you confused
with relief and regret
and indifference

a different time

maybe
I'll always be trying to finish
the second half
of that glass of wine

CENTERED STARS

it turns out
the moon was never full

it was all in our heads
its phases ended
with curves and water slides

and beneath it
I lie on my back sometimes still
remember the way we'd stop and say
we just couldn't go on like this
needed a break a rest
knowing all that meant
we chose to take it literally
for then
we'd collapse
on sidewalks
on the concrete in parking lots
in the fields behind our houses hidden
in the corner aisle of a department store
nobody ever went down but us

it's different now
I still seep into the ground

but I had to replace you with something
and I'm still not sure if those somethings
are better or worse for me than you were
but we self-medicate the way they taught us to self-soothe

the way withered sunflowers and car exhaust fumes
will always remind me of you

the way I tried night after night
to forget what we knew
we'd never be able to hold onto

I'll hold onto those crumpled
dried up fragile petals

I have tucked into the chest
under my bed
the one

I never let anybody in

CINNAMON CLOVES

I wish I'd never taken you
through the door that leads to nowhere
and I wish I'd never said
I'd banish the monsters on the other side
I'm not strong enough for that
so I pulled you back out of the basement
and instead we whispered across ornaments
and the crumbs of broken cookies
about the way we were more afraid
of next year than last

christmas was scattered all over
and you wrote your suicide note
on the back of plaid wrapping paper

I wrote mine in the snow
because I didn't know
that you weren't still as devoted
to trudging through
as I was
so later
mine melted and yours

was framed forever
on the back of my eyelids

"frosty the snowman"
is the saddest song I ever heard

I always thought that

GLYCOL CYANIDE

my grandma broke my heart the night she called
to scream and curse at me for abandoning her

and she broke it again when she called back crying
begging me to forgive her

a breaking heart I admit is a luxury it means
there's something in there still beating

and you need a reminder of that
occasionally
the safest days
consume you anyway

there are procedures breaking all the time
there is deadness in our eyes
there is very little you can guess in this world
swim with the sharks and
watch the minnows eat you alive

everything's coming up thorns
and I'm mourning the way it hurts
when they shrivel up and leave

take off your gloves and watch
as your fingers bleed
there's no need for bandages
our bodies have a remarkable way
of fixing what we care the least about

and if you're out of options
and you've run out of both blame and shame
remember that a little blood
never hurt anybody usually we all know
we're more like plants than animals

shovel dirt into a hill
eat flowers until you've gotten your fill

and remember
when your walls are up and impenetrable
the way it felt
when your grandma called you crying

CRYSTALIZED INNOCENCE

I'll confess that I crave
walking on untouched snow
under the moon alone
and I know
there's a metaphor here
about solitude and destruction
but I'd rather you believe
it's one of beauty

it's not that I'm pretending
to be someone I'm not
it's that I'm trying to protect you
from a side of me you don't want to see

please please forget me

let me retell you the story
of little red riding hood
I am little red making bad decisions
I am the lumberjack trying my best to save this mess
I am the grandma who never showed
but mostly I am the wolf in a dress because
sheepskin is too obvious

I am the stones

I am the axe

maybe I contain multitudes
maybe I contain constant decisions
to hide behind a red hood
and good intentions

LIAR

spinning there in the dim light
pictures pirouetting off half-pipes
I finally started to understand why

that was the first night
my schema was shattered

jagged pieces of cognition
lying on the floor broken
synapses bleeding out
butchering their rapport
I could almost hear my parents telling me: look
this is why we don't run around barefoot

but I'm a grown up now
no one to lift me up out of this
clean it up while I stand in the kitchen
until they tell me it's safe again
that spring night was just the end
of the beginning of so many stupid mistakes

getting tired of taking what I can get
time propelling me ahead and tossing

me back again face contorted crooked grin
numbers on the clock
like a tightrope held taught by am and pm
like the way fighting with my mom
always makes me feel like I'm twelve years old again

and yesterday I dropped my dignity
and picked up a bunch of shit with it
grocery lists of bread and oranges
reminders of renewing my license
self-referential bits and tweets I never sent
sorted through the madness
in a last-ditch attempt to find what matters

but matches made in hell
always burn up too fast

so I slapped a cast on my glass schema
and carried it down the hall to bed
it asked me for forgiveness
and I said your severed neurons need the night

and unlike the alleged george washington I can tell a lie
but I try my best not to
I've never chopped down a tree
just stepped on my own schema and you see

there's no harm done there to anybody but me
I'm good at all kinds of damage

I used to try to write without lies
because they have a way of
sneaking up on you and being misused
until they tie you up to electrodes and beat you

and poetry is a lot like nonfiction
except none of it is true

I don't trust people
who don't have trust issues
so excuse me for asking you
to forget you ever read this
there's a messiness to broken
lines that makes me want to cry
and I sometimes wonder why we are
putting our bodies up for critique
just by existing we talked about this the other night
the flame from the citronella candle flickering
conversing about just how much there is
we are unwaveringly unsure of

and of course I look above
for answers and excuses

an abusive attempt
to make the winding world level

what does it say that we bargain with God
but make a deal with the devil?

appeals burning our lips regardless
there is so much I want but never get

demons will play russian roulette
until they catch you but
they never lurk in dungeons or grandiosity

demons only lurk in the spaces between
comfort and curiosity

II.

FOOL'S SILVER

of course I think less of you
now but don't worry too much
about it

you shouldn't take my opinion
as anything other than stardust or
an imogen's secret

I want you to eat poetry
off of my tongue

it's up to the gutless
to get this going again

these days what matters most
is avoiding your attention I think
and only screaming inside my head

you're too pathetic to see straight
and I am tired of pretending
that's not the case

tired of pretending like I don't want to
wear high heels down dark alleys

I was gonna write my mom a letter
telling her what you did but
I don't wanna break her heart any more
than it already is

some doors open when you force them
and their splinters never leave your skin

I'm jumping over every pothole
in a tear-stained velvet dress
screaming in the dark

you should hear some of the things
men have said to me,
ma

FAKED CONVERSATIONS

we were playing never have I ever when you asked me
I smiled and sipped my drink said I didn't
see the ocean until I was eighteen but
I still know an iceberg when I see one

we are watering fertilizer with diesel fuel and
expecting flowers to grow feigning surprise
at the inevitable explosion

this is a sinking ship, baby, better learn
to swim with a flute of champagne in your left hand
toast to the holes in the boat and
give your heart away while you still can

I've been sifting through the sand
searching for my half-buried mistakes
cutting my hands on broken shells and memories

this is where we break our necks in solidarity
we see ourselves in so many stories

if you look closely enough you might
learn too much about me
put our secrets on the page
with slant rhymes and line breaks and pray
that makes them pretty enough to be palatable

you left me with the ghosts of fireworks
in this foggy night sky I drive around
just to catch them sometimes

by lamplight I'll flip through the left collections
pretend like it's a conversation
tuck myself in for the night whisper
goodbyes soaked in bitter wine

been spending too much time picking up my phone
and putting it down again
you taught me callousness but
I never did learn my full lesson

and nobody was surprised when I realized
I had forgotten your question
but it was okay because you had barely stirred and
I knew you never really cared about my answer

SPRING AWAKENINGS

take me back to six years old again when
nothing not even our skeletons were
permanent. she caught me one night said stand up

brush the chalk dust off your hands. I heard
you had some questions for me so scuff
the pastel scars and get talking.

I have always been so needy when
it comes to affection but I don't have
to tell you that. the other day I got a text

from a ghost and she seemed more alive
than most people who pass by me
on the other side of the street. it must be so exhausting

always having to reassure my fucked-up brain. yesterday
I told you I was trying and that was a lie but
this time I mean it. I'm working on not becoming

a robot but thinking with your soul gets a
little harder the older you get. I already told you
I would sleep on it, this bed of poisoned petals.

tell me, how do you make it out of something
like this without turning more machine than
blood or bones? she said this is how

you tell if someone is empty: curl
them beneath their covers and watch
how long it takes them to unfold.

LOST THINGS

in this picture you're barely holding me in your arms
and we're laughing so hard you'd never know
I was terrified just minutes ago

there are so many things to be afraid of
and I'm not picky

it's true we said we'd take the word
regret out of our vocabulary but
we both know this isn't what we built it up to be

we were gonna be pioneers we said
hike to the top of every hill in this
newly reckoned town

don't tell me you wish you could take it back
did you really think something that started
at a fleetwood mac cover band concert
was destined to last?

neither one of us is coming out of this a savior
but I'll still sing to you as you drive away if you want

you won't be able to hear me but
you will see my lips moving through the glass

and you will wonder what song I chose
the whole way home

CONFETTI CUPS

wore beer logo shirts
but drank vodka tonics
miller and bud didn't cut it that night
gave the boot to the guys
who argued about our truths
climbed too high for them to catch us
brushed up against the tops of trees
grabbed their leaves to levitate
but we slipped and tripped anyway
banged our knees on the concrete
had bruises for weeks
memories stained our skin memories
deep-seated issues that only come up
drunk hiding behind tree stumps
and underneath the trampoline
stoke the sputtering fire
laughter in cascades of carousels
we only begin to break the law when
it won't break any hearts
not innocent ones at least
at least usually
and we only reach
our peak madness
after midnight

THE HALF-LIFE OF DECAY

I hate to romanticize mistakes but
don't you think it's kinder this way?

today I tried to paint a sunset except
everything I make turns out apocalyptic

here I am creating fairy tales out of
what could have been

spinning underneath a roof caving in
don't you think it's a little bit magic?

the way the ceiling scrapes our skin
the way we are playing an unending game

of double dutch among the ruins
this building's crumbs

watch us hang a disco ball off a broken rafter and
catch sparkles on our tongues

COUNTRY CURTAINS

we all want revenge but so many of us
would settle for justice. I'm not talking about logistics
today I am talking to friends through a computer screen

and now there is the hint of a permanent
smiley face on my bedroom wall. I have
made so many casual mistakes. I have
shot at soda cans with a bb gun at close range

and done so much better than the boys did. do you
remember the coveted sticky tac we'd collect
when the teachers let us help them clean out
their classrooms on the last of school? drawing our names
in shaving cream like reverse finger paints.

these are our collective keepsakes. please
marry my memories. sing the vows to the crowd
of ladybugs on my front porch. I told you before

I'm not talking about logistics today. I am
talking through black ink on a white page. I filled

the dent in my wall with toothpaste and I laugh
every time I pass it. please don't kiss me

in the sunken garden. just lie on the ground
beside me and stare at what's left
of the stars. we named the fountain there graceful
martyr. once filled it with water from the bottles
we brought from home because an empty fountain
in the ghost of a lake was the saddest thing

we'd ever seen. I've been over this already.
I'm not talking about logistics today. I'm talking
about you and me and the trace of sharpie on our skin.
did you think if you whispered goodbye it would hurt less?

I recognized every damn one of your tactics. this isn't
about changing the channel or searching for yourself
in a song. this is about the clocks being an hour behind
half the year because I don't know how
the settings work on my car's dashboard. this is about how

I was only supposed to give you a
ride home that first night but you complimented
my commitment to protesting daylight savings time.

this is about a guy at the bar who gave us a dollar when
we were drunk and really wanted to win
the stuffed gingerbread man. this is about a girl jumping out
of the telephone booth before I knew you. this is about
the onion you placed by my bed when I was sleeping
because you read it could help cure colds.

we crashed away with bulleted phrases
of our own private questions
so I'll tell you this:
your worst offense wasn't leaving

the coffee pot empty but it did make the list. we made it out
beautiful but we didn't make it far. kept each other warm &
left a few legends in our wake. I'm not talking about logistics
today. I am swept in the blurriness of both
our mistakes. we were born to be gutter balls
and slippery dance floors and sad songs
in the late morning slipped back into bed.

I've been told I'm an empath but I don't think
I'm a good enough person for that. I wonder if you
ever forgave me for all the things I almost did. take me home
but drive real slow and make sure to turn on the car radio.

listen to the lyrics again before you
change the station. know that broken
blinds still let the light in.

cover them up
with your old flannels.

GOLDEN SAFETY

had a dream last night
that I crushed up my front door lock
and drank it down like a fine powder
a loud nightmare
where I held a key
that opened nothing
I screamed with all that
power of security behind me

and I washed it down with water

cleansed in the sins of muddy sediment
and busted deflated floaties
they never did their job right

and neither did you

I woke up and checked the lock
not because I was afraid
I had consumed it
but because I was afraid
it

had
consumed
me

TEARDROP TRIPS

sometimes I wish you were here again to call me
names to sing me to sleep with rants and hatred
watch me walk away watch me come back
I missed your insults missed your guilt
missed the way I had the upper hand
when we curled our love into fists

I never meant to forget you
I don't miss you but I do
miss all you stood for

I just stopped needing to hold your
heartache stopped letting our tangled tears
dry on my skin tracing the outlines of your skeleton
holding your desire your darkness your fears

but I'll inhale your cigarette breath
for years

take you back to the bridge
where we threw our empty beer cans
and past mistakes at each other

built motes out of baggage
and bad reactions
and sank beneath the blue

that bridge holds all your secrets now
like I used to

our origin story both starts and ends in smoke
and you will always choke down more champagne
than you should
when I'm with you

EMPTY GYMNASIUMS

when I die
bury me like a prom queen
who doesn't want to wrinkle her dress

when you say goodbye
whisper your confessions to me
before they close the lid

but for now
just keep dancing

let's make promises we can't keep
and pretend we've forgotten them in the morning

they cancelled the fourth of july
the year I turned sixteen
something about the risk of burning

I didn't blame you for it
but maybe I should have

I think the moon is so pretty on your face
but you need to know that

if you put me between a rock and hard place
I will cut myself in half to fit

if you chase me to the end of my rope
I will brace myself and let go
because I'd rather break my body than share it

give me a morning glory and play my favorite song
and I will try my hardest not to haunt you

you can decide for yourself
whether to consider that a promise

THE BEST FLOWERS CRY TEARS OF BLOOD

I never even told
my therapist about you
couldn't find the right
parts of speech
for what we used to be
suffocating breaking hitting

but it was nothing
the casual violence of siblings
and close friends

I know the reunions are so
much sweeter in my memory but

aren't the bruises just proof
that we felt something?

when we ripped each other apart
we got to sew ourselves back
together tighter clinging
to each other like

specks of glass near the end
we pulled so hard
we kept for ourselves pieces
of each other's skin and
knuckles and hearts

I only prefer the light because
it's too easy to tell the truth in the dark

IF YOU STUCK THE LANDING

I used to have this reoccurring dream where I
had to choose between saving my grandma or me
an apocalypse abduction or a robbery
but I always woke up before the ending

and to my parents I whisper
"be safe" over and over again
like a prophecy like a prayer

if you're ever unsure whose life
is most intertwined with your own
ask yourself whose name you'd scream
in an emergency

a guy I knew once told me
he felt like God before He flooded the earth
and my only thought was *I wonder*
if I'd make it on the ark

then I spent a tuesday afternoon with a girl I knew
doing gymnastics in my apartment living room
a reunion wrapped up in a death sentence

and still we twirled in the sun beams

twisted the caps off a couple blue moons
caught her eyes as we danced
we said we drink for fun not to cope with our problems

and we laughed
and we laughed
and we laughed

TEMPTING AIR

it was just another one of those nights
when we reeked of whiskey and wine
underneath the burning smell of
vanilla and cigarettes
and budding romance
said looks like
you'll only be in love tonight
and not beloved tonight
read her like the posters
hung up in a room
you'd pay to leave
like last night's texts a little
bit fuzzy like the instructor's manual
after you've already fucked up
everything
I didn't want to be in love that night
or any night
but they'd probably say it happened anyway
I'm always apologizing for what's already been forgotten
but I never regret the things I should
and I know I need to stop dancing on the verge
of this bridge but I love too much

the way it feels to take in the whole city at once
to catch its breath in my lungs
she only inhaled her cigarettes
when I was watching
and I wanted to tell her how basely
I understand that her hands are always cold
and empty
but I was already testing backbends
over the bridge's edge
so instead I told her
never forget how to furnish a mind
with plenty of barstools
and paintings that shine
flicked the cigarette butts off to the side
said if you realize you've picked up
someone else's heart,
you better return it
never fall for whiskey and vanilla,
unless you've earned it, and
if you love something,
burn it

FALSE SHEEP

hitting april means unearthing
the linings of old dresses and
ending the messes I get into night after night

maybe learning how to stop navigating
by pop tabs and tea lights

I should have never taken these too-bright
pictures or at least I should have turned off the flash

act like that doesn't matter
spin me in a circle until the sky blurs and
I can pretend you are someone else
that I'm the type of girl who keeps her promises to trim
around your edges in all her photos

changed your name in my phone to satan
so I'd have some excuse for falling for your tempting

it'd be better for my story if you wore red
but I'm the one in cherry lace

the devil is calling again and again and
I'm always running late

SWEETENED SMOKE SIGNALS

the sun always forgot to come up
mornings after poisoning ourselves
I preferred pink wine and cheap vodka
and you used the tobacco stuffed in
your favorite stupid corn cob pipe
piled on each other's words
for good measure

said so much shit I never even meant
you would beg me
I would never admit it
sometimes I made the bed with you still in it
sang a symphony of forbidden words
the guilt of skeletons cracking
lacking the indifference

the false security of seat belt buckles
and stepping over cracks
of studying of eating before you leave for the bar
of trying hard taking pictures
clipping coupons of saying I love you

take it back
wish I could
can't say I actually would

if God granted me the do-overs
I'm always begging for
maybe I'd still fuck it up
all over again

maybe I like the excuses for the distances
I put between you and me before you vanished
disappeared

I don't miss so much of us
never wanted our skin to touch or
our friends to meet or
our lives to intertwine but

sometimes I bite the teeth marks
you left behind on your favorite
stupid
corn cob pipe

WHEN YOU ASKED ME TO LOOK AT AN OLD PICTURE OF MYSELF AND SPEAK TO IT, I HAD NO IDEA WHAT TO SAY

I will always remember the first time I was told
to suck it in
trying on the dress she bought me and I don't
think she noticed my face turning red or
my body sinking in probably
because she'd done so much
shrinking herself that by nine when I hadn't yet learned
to feel bad about taking up
the space the places that were rightfully mine
I seemed too much to her already

I don't blame her
all that much but
I do see now I shouldn't
have been the one ashamed should've spoken up that day
should've walked away
didn't even want that dress in the first place

it was ugly

I don't have to write about what it's like
to hate what you see in window reflections
and the surfaces of still waters
we are all wounded and war-torn
from going into battle with our bodies
evading now
tired of hating what I see
in the backs of spoons candle lids other people's sunglasses

I'm not sure if my body and mind
are enemy lines or if this is friendly fire
gonna make a liar out of my old self
somehow want to love
the person I want to be and the person I am now

still masquerading still in training still times
I read my words
don't remember who that girl was other times
it's such a short distance between
her and me
it stings

WE ARE THE NOOSE AND THE SCISSORS

there's no need to worry
about the skeletons
in your garden
they'll help the flowers grow
you gave me forget-me-nots
your way of saying you
knew me already
knew the way I'd see you
everywhere after

startling at the ice maker
the way we celebrated
clinking glasses of cold champagne

you knew you'd always have me
tangled up in stems and suffocating

said we couldn't live like this
our hearts handcuffing our fists

technically

our love died before the flowers did
but what an omen
we floated for so long on passion
mistaking destruction for infatuation

tracing lines across each other's throats

I will always believe
people can change

but I know
they usually don't

CADAVERS

there are some structures
that crack under the pressure
this town's full of foundations
that made a suicide pact
and the bones of their buildings
still haunt the alleys that swallowed them
broken beer bottles scattered among
the cigarette ashes
and receipts so worn
you can't even read the buyer's secrets
the paths that get you to the cemetery
the fastest are like ghost tours
of these abandoned properties
all you need are knives and knuckles
and the guts it takes
to fill the skeletons in your wake

STATIC SENDING

the smoldering inside us is
only an issue
when we flicker dead and bruised

didn't forget I promised to call you
or maybe even write
but midnight lights always shine
brighter and

even the mailman
breaks down sometimes

I'd never tell you
you are background
noise at this point

drank all your tequila
bled on your floor
didn't clean it up

trouble marked there in red
another mess I left you with

another excuse
for some other time

I'm hoping to visit soon
but it's such a long drive

SENTIMENTAL SUNSETS

I know a guy who never watches
the last episode of
any of his favorite shows
because he already knows he's not
ready for the inevitable end

and I guess it got me thinking about
trapezing through finales clinging desperately
to splintered rungs and really
closure is for break ups and deaths

yet here I am again
scared
of so many things
that I love

I draw temporary tattoos with felted ink
on my skin because
I am afraid of both pain and permanence
so of course I like the sidewalks in the fall most of all

and tomorrow when most of the world is tucked in at home
I will blow a kiss to the old office
and the semi-abandoned gym
trip over loose bricks on the hunt for some madness

I will allow for one more round of this hideous self-
indulgence
at least until our shadows grow long and innocent again

I will always break my stride to make leaves crunch
beneath my boots to tuck secrets away
in my faded denim jackets to try to be thankful
for the forced goodbye of sunshine

to think of fitzgerald and smile

it is autumn
and everything is dead
but I
am alive

MY BIGGEST FEAR IS BEING AFRAID

been talking a lot of shit for an indecisive
hypocrite without a sense of direction
but what a curse to save the worst for myself

how ironic that they
call it a comforter

the other night I spent two hours
vacuuming one square foot of my apartment
and unpeeling bandages I knew
would never stick to my skin
but this morning I am twirling bare
feet brushing nothing dreaming about
gas station tulips and abstract announcements

finally taught myself how to start measuring ounces
but I've already forgotten how to divide fractions and

the attraction of drinking is that it's
the most alive and the most dead you ever feel

sometimes I do ballet in circles around

my own grave other times I sprint from it
and all the times between I spend
on my scratched knees clawing at the dirt
begging the trap door to open
one day I will swallow enough future flowers
to reach the bottom and my skeleton will sing
the lyrics to all the hymns I learned when I was six
and the sheryl crow duet we'd karaoke to
before we even knew what it meant
to still love someone you'd chosen to leave

don't mistake me for a friendly enemy
I have sewn too many stones into the linings of my pockets
it's not that I want so much of it it's that I want
to want it but can never seem to get that far

once at a bar I overheard a guy say he liked the idea
of sloths in australia and I wanted to ask him
so many questions but they all fell from my lips and
drowned in my gin and tonic

I am constantly in love with ideas and never actualities
a leech stuck to my own body I think maybe
if I say I'm sorry enough someday

I'll be able to forgive the world
and us

I always forget to recycle my wine bottles but
I say my best prayers when I'm drunk

bury me ten feet deep
six just isn't enough

THE BURDEN OF EXISTING

I used to wear overalls of blue denim
stitched flowers gathered at the hem but
we are in a fashionless summer so I haven't
seen them in years

thought about telling the guy next to me
at the cemetery this we are
rows apart staring at the new water tower we
thought was a silo before they finished it

he is clinging to his smudged sunglasses but
his bottle of whiskey must have gotten too heavy to carry
so he dropped it off by the same gravestone
I once saw somebody do a line of coke off of maybe
he reminds me of emotional symmetry
like waking up and remembering
you cried yourself to sleep or
fighting the unfairness of how no one told you
everything even the pitch of your grandmother's voice
would change in the end

all of it is easier in past tense
and I have been paying for kindness my entire life

I broke your candle seven months ago
cut myself with the shards of it
one or two of them

you will never know if it was an accident
I will never know why the carpet didn't
catch fire I never

trim the wicks I like
the way the ashes look I am

running from medicine from the midnight
devil on his crumbling chair
read the inscriptions stitched together
like a poem begging
for hindsight I am

mad at all the beautiful lines I didn't write
there are so many beautiful lines

ABOUT THE AUTHOR

Katie Holtmeyer lives, writes, and teaches in Missouri. She is a pushcart-nominated author, and her poetry has appeared in Vast Chasm, Stanchion Zine, and The Shore, among others. You can find more of her work at katieholtmeyer.com.

ABOUT UNSOLICITED PRESS

Unsolicited Press is based out of Portland, Oregon and focuses on the works of the unsung and underrepresented. As a womxn-owned, all-volunteer small publisher that doesn't worry about profits as much as championing exceptional literature, we have the privilege of partnering with authors skirting the fringes of the lit world. We've worked with emerging and award-winning authors such as Shann Ray, Amy Shimshon-Santo, Brook Bhagat, Kris Amos, and John W. Bateman.

Learn more at unsolicitedpress.com. Find us on twitter and instagram.